Thoughts Alight Poetry

A DOORWAY TO A SECRET GARDEN

KAWTAR ELMRABTI

EC Publishing LLC
11100 SW 93rd Court Road, Suite 10-215
Ocala, Florida 34481-5188, USA

Ordering Information:
Quantity sales. Special discounts are available on quan-
tity purchases by corporations, associations, and others. For
details, contact the publisher at the address above.

www.ecpublishingllc.com
info@ecpublishingllc.com
+1 (352) 234-6201

Printed in the United States of America

Poet's note

This book is more than a book, it's a meadow full
of thoughts, alight with hope, love, inspiration,
sadness, meditation, ambition and these are the seeds
that grew throughout my life. Welcome to my sweet
meadow. Hopefully you will appreciate your journey
within the land of my thoughts. Once you turn your
dreams into plans a whole new realm of possibilities
and sparks opens up to you. Each chapter holds the
symbol of petal blossoming into a thought given to
you in the hope to inspire you.

To the beaming souls who inspired me and encouraged me to reach my dreams, Arista, Agninda, Kiana, Jessica, Elise,Caitlin, Yasmin Cabak, Sophia, Shaima, Angelina, Melanie, Lili Reinhart, Cole Sprouse,Melissa Ponzio,Tamare,Fatima,Gladys, Bill Johnson. Thank you for your ever beaming support and kindness towards me. My creative journey flows from the seeds of hope these precious souls gave me. I cherished them and turned them into creative plans.

'The natural flights of the human mind are not from pleasure to pleasure but from hope to hope.'

- Samuel Johnson

Petals:

Love Thoughts

Love is an essence flowing into our souls through many forms. Mine was mainly flowing from inspiration of stories I have read and witnessed in many ways.

Me and my shadow

Wherever I go, my love for you never stops to flow
Wherever we go, our love never ceases to glow
For when our eyes meet we set our hearts aflame
Our souls are one and the same
Balancing each other out like a melody and its tempo
I can sense your glow
I can sense your motions
Our bodies moving in perfect sync
Our gazes full of emotions
Enhancing our glorious link
Like two entangled strings on a guitar
We never stop shining together like a shooting star
Becoming my shadow
My footprints in the snow
For you belong to me
Like lovers belong in pair
Like stars and air
As lovers we cross the sunlight in one shape
Being the entity of our strong bright love
Our shadows meeting among a beautiful meadow
Being the abode of our love, our blooming feelings
Me and my shadow
Flying away together
Crossing light and darkness
In perfect balanced blissfulness
Me and my shadow fell in love
Once dreaming above the aura of true love
Now diving into true love together

Love is Louder

Love is louder than the sun's boiling sparks
Louder but also brighter
And prettier
Love is an endless spark
Love is louder than any fears
It rings in our ears and hearts
As a powerful bell
Covering every sound of pain
Love is louder than every Lion roars
Love has its own roar
Filled with smoothness
Bliss, happiness, it's a glowing roar
Love is louder than Time running fast
Love evolves and shines at a fast pace
Love is timeless and endless
Love is louder than the earth spinning around
Love is this glowing constellation in our hearts
And above us
Love is louder than any fireworks
Its flame burns brighter
An endless sparkling flame
In the sky of our lives
Love is louder than any disease
Its power heals everything
Like a magic wind
Love is a mystery to be explored
And cherished

An Adventure

As I gaze into your beautiful eyes
I smile feeling your love inside my heart
Your love fills my heart up
I am smitten with you
Your elegance, your stance
My heart so gently pounds
With you I'm so smitten
Tangled by silly cuteness
Like a ball of red wool
Chased by a kitten
First crush of emotion
Led to deepest devotion
In a field of poppies
Your dress flowing through the air
As I marvel into your allure
We travel together
Painting the silhouette of our love
Our senses intertwined
Like two white doves
Soaring in the blue skies
Our senses embracing the soul of this earth
As we kiss under many skies, many suns, many moons
Of all shapes and shades
Like my admiration for you
Together, we take life as a journey
Giving life to a never ending love
For we are endless explorers
Across the clouds, the oceans, the fields
We cherish each other's flaws
From the inside out

For our love is raw
Unlike any other
A glowing tether
Spreading in all the places
We ventured
In you I found the silhouette of Love
I see journeys in your palms
Adventures awaiting in your smile
The gleam of your eyes
My ever constellation

Red Roses' hues

In you I found a home
A path to endless adventures
In beautiful landscapes, I used to roam
Now taken into lovers strolls
By your side
Your eyes shine so intensely
The midday sun seems so dark
I would telescope the sheen of your gaze
As an astronomer admires the night sky
Revelling in this beauty
Stumbling across the magnificence
That is your gentle soul
Our love's like Spring
Colorful, fresh
Your affection,my wanderlust
Capturing your beauty in meadows
Among a wonderland of snow
A flash of light, then a fest of colors
Framing the brightest eyes
Staring at my soul
My heart filled with delight
Behind sweet peach lips
A smile reflected a smile
Our love, a rose garden
Gazing at your creamy silk skin
As the sun shows its keenest love to the snow
When we're together
Loss of air, loss of sense,loss of self
Two bodies in one
For we are each other's gravity

You are the stars of my galaxy
Snowflakes on your golden hair
Rose petals turning into sparkles
Whirling around our shinny silhouettes
Our tangled lust for life
Giving birth to an endless love
Like the four seasons circle

Unique quintessence

You are my special light
Turning on inside me
When all my creativity fades away
You are that glowing inward beam of mine
That strengthens my life, enlightens my soul within
You and I
Immersed in the fairy tale that is our love story
Feeling each other's warmth
In this winter wonderland
Beneath the blankets of white snow
Grey clouds engulfing us in the love
That is the warmth
Of our limbs intertwined together
Your dazzling allure
My everlasting muse
As I capture your beauty
I write sonnets upon your essence
Made of purity and stardust
My love for you is infinite
Kissing your soul
As we shape our love's quintessence

Clarity

When everything is a blur
Your light green eyes, my clarity
New clarity sparks
Capturing your Beauty
So readily, so heartily
Snowflakes on your golden hair
In a blissful tranquility
As my heart is ablaze
Comfort enfolds me
The way your eyes love my soul
A Beam unlike any other
Tracing the sparks of our Love
When you look at me
My soul feels alive and bright
The soft glow of your eyes
Greater than the brightest stars
Ever to grace the midnight sky
The treasured glow within them
Embracing me
Shaping the colorful horizon
Of our Love
Your light green eyes
My ever constellation
As a flash of light
Mirrors my endless admiration

Ocean's echo

I see journeys in your palms
Adventures awaiting in your smile
The silhouette of our love
Defying the sunlight
Our love, the palette of a sunset
Hands intertwined
We strolled under the orange sunset
Under green palm trees
Gently afloat a clear blue ocean
Feeling the sweet warmth of your palms
As the wind embraces the sheen of your hair
I long to run my fingers in your golden locks
For you are my siren, enchanting my heart
Graceful allure in this wavy white dress of yours
You re my perfect palette of sunset
The green of your eyes
Your sun kissed skin
As I lay in the sand, taking a picture of you
Our embrace, the finest purest melody of joy
For I would surf on top of your tallest waves
You are my shore
I am your sandy bay
We are the ocean's greatest bliss
The flaring shades of our love will endlessly sway
The touch of your lips on mine
A moving sea between the shores of our souls
You are my piece of paradise
My ocean, always filling my heart with songs of serenity
Far away the ocean sounds and resounds
Like the echoes of your name in my heart

In this moment
Sunlight on our silhouettes
We end each other's sentences with our breaths
For we are fluent in true love
I see the future in your glistening eyes
As I hold you ever closer to my beating heart
You and I
Brought together by the flow
Of Fate's turquoise tides

Sand and pearls

You're the fish
I wrote in the sand
Holding your hand
In your scent, I relish
As we softly caress
Gazing at the rushing waves
Inhaling your breath as we kiss
Feeling a love so stellar so pure
As we lay in the soft sand
Our entwined souls
Shaping the most beautiful pane of glass
In the Sun rays
Your eyes are pearls
Defying the crystal waters and silky skies
Our kisses, the air that flows from cosmic beyond
Whispering words of love coated with passion
Two hearts laced into one
In you, I found my starry sky
To explore endlessly
From every beat of my heart
I cherish our love as one pearl
Sitting quietly by the sea
Your soul, mine to endlessly cherish
For you are the fish
In the sea of my life
My quintessential siren

Sunset Palette

'Allow me to lose myself in your constellations'
You once whispered to me
Through my photography
I capture the gleam of your beauty
Sun flickered upon your eyes
Scintillating as the seas
Through my lens
In your eyes, I see the sheen
Of a thousand swooning moons
For you are my sunshine
Every morning I see you rise
Lying down with you
Your sweet touch, the horizon of my soul
Eyes glistening in the crack of sunlight
Sneaking in between the pearly curtains
Sunlight dancing on your tanned skin
The green of your eyes
Like emeralds reflecting the sun
You have my soul mesmerized
In your eyes, I see the very hue of life
The palette of a sunset
Allow me to lose myself in your lovely skies
Your passion, my red sun
Every poem I write flow from you
I write of your golden skin under the soft sunlight
For I want to spend the rest of my life
Counting the stars on your skin
I don't have a telescope that can see through flesh and bones
You have to speak me your constellations
Our entwined love

A whole universe inside of each other
Filled with starlight
They say 'love is written in the stars'
Ours is threaded between the stars

Love's breeze

Watching the sun rising in the sky
Relaxing on the beach, just you and I
A cool gentle breeze blowing upon our face
As we stared into the depths of space
The waters so calm and blue
As the seagulls above us flew
We sway,tanned skin and sea breeze kisses
Melodic motions to the rhythm
Of sunlit waves
As we walk along the deserted sand
Our arms swing gently, hand in hand
To the graceful rhythm of the waves
Sunlight in your hair
I, enchanted by you
The beautiful sparkly mermaid that you are
As our love alights your pretty face
I feel our heartbeats starting to race
Without another soul around
We lay our blanket on the ground
As I watch the sunlight reflect in your eyes
Deep emerald green
Sunkissed smiles coming together
Like the tide around us, our passion arises
Your kisses tasting salty
The sparkling sand massaging our toes
Clouds and colors painted across the sky
Complimenting our enamored eyes
Violet, rose, bluest of blues
Peach with vanilla hues
Love-filled palette made for two

Your presence, my gravity
With you, I stay afloat
The clouds of my happiness
Filled with smoothness
Your hair between my fingers
Everything is blue around us
For you my darling
My heart is crimson like fire
On this beach there is but one sound
Our hearts beating together
For we are sunkissed lovers

Ethereal Sheen

Oasis that you are
Much like a water sage to the mirage of my soûl
My tongue swells for your neverending glory
Gleaming golden locks at the nape
of your neck
Your silver allure, high and mighty
Your sheen is divine
My Aphrodite of ethereal Beauty
Let me taste your subtle charms
Languish in my warming arms
For you are my greatest ally
My purpose is to steer the sea
Yours to light my sky
My internal beams, only you can see
Smiles gleamed in the moment
Your perfume, my exotic zeal

Magnetic attraction
Unchangeable is the Love within our souls
Like perfect polished silver
Our Love, patterned with glory
My Ares of ethereal elegance
Sculptor of my universe
Your heartbeat lulling me
Into the finest hymn of bliss
Our souls pulled together
Perceived in hues of white and gold
By Heaven's glory
Our eyes glazed with true adoration

Changing tide

The world was a stranger to me
Until you helped me change the tide
In this vast world
I travelled a lonely path
Until my soul saw you
You were my oasis
When I was thirsty for adventures
You and I
Intertwined our paths
My love for you shaped my world
Your eyes,my constellation
Your shiny presence
My fragrance of happiness
You are my morning light
With you
The darkest paths seem alight
You fill my soul with sunshine
My heart with tender care
I have read countless books
But you are the most beautiful book
By your side
I travelled length and width
Of greatest bliss
Your mind ignited mine
To form Love's sparks
Defying the moon's brightness
When you take my band
I feel like a dove
You are my world
I long to spin you like a globe

To discover pieces of you
Unlock your soul's secrets
Our intimacy, a galaxy unlike any other
Where our emotions sparkle
For the moon swoons over our Love
Our adventure, so stellar so pure
Connection lasting a lifetime
No measure of time or space
Could come between our entwined souls
Two affiliated beaming souls
Threaded between the greatest constellations
Our Love's silhouette, a lunar beam
For you my love
My eyes endlessly gleam

Intertwined hearts

Your embrace is my whole realm
I miss all of you
The way our eyes soften and dilate when we kiss
Your fingertips setting my palm on fire
All of our precious moments
Embedded within my heartbeats
For my ears are eternally wedded to yours
Strolling down landscapes of beauty
Longing to feel your warmth
Smitten with your perfume
Your natural glow
For I cherish our love
With every gifted sunrise
Taking our love's essence wherever I go
A love carved into my heart
Intertwined with my soul
Written from the start
 You and I
Like woven pieces of ribbon
Connected from opposite ends of the globe
Our hearts perfectly laced
Through the distance
I remain longing in our shared kisses
Till we find each other
Our bodies will touch in a magic sensation
Gasping for more air
Holding each other tight
Never letting go
Swaying in each other's warmth
Till midnight

We'll share many splendored kisses
Under the moonlit sky
Our synced hearts
Infinitely intertwined
Our love a stellar silhouette
Unlike any other

A Fresh Dawn

Light of a fresh dawn
Giving birth to a new day
By your side
The fresh air filled with our Love's fragrance
Ready to conquer the vast world
Distance eroded
When our souls collide
As the sunlight glimmer at your cheek
In your ever loving gaze
I see the light of many shades
Glinting its spectrum of delight
Right into my soul
In this sun filled day
Our entwined hearts sway
To a blissful ode
My heart pronounced for you
Your spirit flows like a poem
On the lightened path of my life
Souls collided
Casting an ever shining love
Like no other
Together, our hearts rhyme
With Nature's symphony
Welcoming a new day
Light of a fresh dawn
I, enfolded with your scent
The birds singing to our shining bond

A Blissful pace

When we nap together
Your tiny breaths
Are like love songs to my heart
Our moments of laziness
Filled with perfect bliss
Your chest, my safest place
Our breaths dancing
In the same pace
Your soul united with mine
The candle light flickers with our intimacy
Celeste bodies colliding in great allure
Cradle me to the song of our Love
Make me a perfect pillow of your chest
For you are my home
You and I
Anchored lovers
Basking in our sparkling bond
Made of blissful waves
Feeling each other's grace
Your thumb tracing circles on my back
Adventurers by day
Moonlight lovers by night

Here and now

Two hearts linked together by a lovely sunlight
We strolled the rain filled streets of Paris
The city shimmers in the sparks of our Love
Breathing the romantic night air
Wrapped in each other's arms
The moonlight shining all around us
Kisses of tenderness
The hymn of our tangled happiness
In the city of Love
Exchanging vows
"Je t'aime de tout mon coeur"
In the here and now
You're my forever
Mon petit coeur

A Vast Horizon

For years I went on a lonely adventure
To find my soulmate on a wide barren desert
Meeting you was like finding
A vast paradise
To explore endlessly
Our love, a unique gravity
For I feel dizzy in your love
Your eyes, my heavenly abode
You spin me in circles
In an infinite loop of joy
Together we defy the law of physics
Your body, my sublime hemisphere
Infinite time and space
To explore endlessly
Your gaze, my everbeaming horizon
A constellation unlike any other
Your presence, so stellar so pure

My love you give me ethereal bliss
Our entwined souls, luminescent
Dazzling the stars above
In each kiss
Our lips invent a new language
Words spoken only between us
Passionate shiny clouds
Emerging between us
Your lips, writing the greatest verses
Making my heart soar
In a state of delirium
Late night, early morning

Luminescent hearts
Bonded for eternity
With joyful kisses
Emanating a spectrum
Of sparkles in any space we stay in
As my heartbeats sing the verses
'You carry my heart in yours'

A Golden Embrace

Her beautiful face falling on the ground
His soul drowned in a painful wound
Everything fell apart
Their tethered hearts remained intact
For they have an unspoken connection
Filled with powerful devotion
She plunged into a tormenting silence
He plunged into a whirlwind of violence
Both entangled in the sound barrier
When she was a warrior in the painful silence
He was a sparkling hero in the depth of darkness
When she was hopeless
He promised to be her savior
Holding her hand through agonizing pain
Her screams breaking windows
His fiery devotion breaking doors
Leading restless wars
Her shivering body trapped in a hell hole
Screaming her name like a wolf's howl
His heart flying to her rescue
His voice, a healing presence
Erasing her past storms
'Let me save you' he gracefully whispered
His whisper, a soothing lullaby to her heart
His golden eyes gazing at her face
Her smile, his inner peace
Where dark steams and painful screams ruled
Here's the sheen of his Golden Embrace
Long gone are the thunderous screams
Only remains their ardent love

Among the meadow

Two souls destined to be together
Once met under a grey sky
In the meadow of Inverness
Their hearts bounded
Into a fever
Setting their hearts ablaze
Enchanted by each other's gleam
Their union, a golden glow
Taken into the unknown path
Of Love's tides
She became his white dove
When heavens disappeared into a roar
Her glowing wings kept him ashore
Soaring above the depth of darkness
Their love, a glowing shield
Against the wrath of demons
Her healing touch, his safe haven
When his horizon was full of dark ravens
His loving dove spread seeds of hope
Chasing each other's heart in the distance
Facing the waves of agony
Their battle, a fest of elegance
For underneath the waves of hell
A fiery devotion binding their hearts
Into one beaming soul
Crossing the waves of hell as a shadow
Swirling under the moonlight like a golden glow
Weary eyes longing for each other
Now resting forever
In their glorious togetherness

Among the meadow of Inverness
Where lips meet in a blissful dance
Among the radiant meadow
Filled with the sheen of their true love
Dancing with the doves
Of heavens above

Love's Ribbon

Without you my days were empty
Without your presence
Your shining stance
My heart's light fades away
Into the dull clouds of my sadness
Wishing for that emptiness to fly away
Until the merry day
I felt your presence
The vivid colors of your soul
Your precious gaze
Turned my scenery
Into a shimmering horizon
Stare into my eyes
So deeply, so sweetly
The kindness and love behind your smile
Lacing my heart with Love's Ribbon
'It's good to see you' you whisper
Oh so gently
My heart suddenly taken into a blissful melody
For there are songs in your eyes
Singing lullabies to my soul
Your voice lit up my heart
With utter happiness
In this sunlit space
Our feelings low
In perfect harmony
Smiling till our eyes glow together

Fireworks in the meadow

When they entered the meadow it was a sight to behold
Kisses spreading flashes of rainbow
Lips sealed within the daylight
Pink roses swaying to a smooth melody
Melody of pure beauty
Two souls soaring into bliss
Her white cloak, the wings unfolding their pure love
Within the meadow they found their home
Her cloak, a white picket fence
Symbol of their union
Their shining souls, the roof of their hearts
Two hearts purely smitten
Where their light shines forever
Made of the strongest hearts

Soothing Gravity

You have my heart in the palm of your hand
Your beauty so bright and warm
Shining through the darkest storms
Your eyes sparkling like the stars above
When I look through them
I feel like I'm soaring high
My love for you is pure and true
The sweet sound of your voice
Makes my heart pound
So soft and clear
Like the sound of our synced beating hearts
For I am your armor
Meant to protect you from any harm
Like you always been to me, a lucky charm

You set my heart ablaze
When I cross your loving gaze
For you are my soothing gravity
When I'm drifting into darkness
In you I find my lighthouse
Guiding me into a calm shore
My trembling hands
My shivering mind
Find balance in your warm embrace
The caress of your hand sending blissful shivers to my spine
For you are mine
My one and only
The surging of our souls
Keeps us safe
When your gentle kiss landed on my hand

I felt our beaming auras
Spreading the seeds of our ardent love
Into the seven seas
Into the seven skies
Till the infinity of fairy realms

Under the moonlight

She swung from a star
He hung from a crescent moon
Their entwined souls swaying together
Under the moon's beam
She is the glowing sapphire
Guiding him into the sparkling seas
Her voice, his soothing melody
His voice, her calming sweetness
Tethered like the moon and stars
They cross darkness together
Unspoken connection lacing their hearts
Into a beaming string
The moonlight mirrors the flare of their love
Tangled pain, tangled joy
Their light fading together
Their triumph shining together
At the brim of dawn
Their devotion endlessly shimmers
Sparkles of their love
Twirling above the moon's beam
Like shiny dandelion petals
In the sweet daylight

Leap of Faith

When he stood on the edge of a cliff
Where the abysses of despair
And darkness lay below
A warm blow came
Soothing his bleeding heart
On a sunlit day his eyes landed on a vivid soul
Unlike any other
Fierce, pure and vibrant
She was a source of great light
Among the pain he felt
For she was his sunbeam
When his mind was dim
Hands touching, beaming smiles
Made sparks circle their silhouettes
Twinkles in their eyes
Pure innocent love blossomed
Flying to a secret sky
Binding their fates for eternity
Names engraved in each other's hearts
Like the endless sheen of the stars
Becoming each other's sunbeam
Facing the darkest tides
She pushed him to the abyss of belief
Becoming the thief of his heart
Stealing his pain
Her vivid spirit ran in his veins
Merging of a two brave souls
Making the stars shine brighter
Among the surrounding darkness
Shouting his sheer love for her

Green emerald eyes embracing his soul
Lips colliding in solemn bliss
Opening their hearts into a whirl of chances
They became each other's balance
In a world of chaos
Their love soared into the sweet embrace of Faith

A Candlelit Miracle

Under the christmas tree
Star-flecked eyes meeting
In perfect harmony
In your eyes, I saw the sheen of the stars
For your loving gaze is my galaxy
Candlelit room
Our souls merged into one
For a brief moment
Mine to cherish forever
No words spoken
Love spoke on our behalf
Fluttering eyes
Tracing enamored smiles
In this blissful moment
Of two souls merging together
Creating sparkles
Unlike any other
Blowing one candle in unison
We are soulmates
You are my saving grace
Your freckles, perfect constellations
To my eyes
To my soul
Under the christmas tree
A miracle came upon me

Glorious Venue 1

In this glorious venue
I felt love's hues
A path leading to eternal vows
Smiles on all these faces
Ready to witness True Love's glow
Until I saw you on the other side
Of this beaming alley
Your gaze made me blush
Like Roses in the Spring air
Admiring each other's allures
Basking in the sunlight
For I believe one day
I'll be your fair lady
Awaiting you on this beaming alley
Where our love will ascend
Will grow its shining seeds
Alongside your greatness
We are budding life mates
For now
And I shall rejoice on this bond
We share, so powerful, so epic
In this glorious venue
Our True Love reached the light
Of a beaming future
Awaiting us

Glorious Venue II

Sunshine radiates through your hair
In this glorious venue
I only have eyes for you
Scarlet-haired princess
Your hair perfectly complimenting
Your beaming smile
Animating my soul
With utter happiness
Your enchanting gaze
Burning away my loneliness
For you are my Scarlet-haired lady
Your lips a vibrant red
Defying the sheen of the sunset
In the summer days
I fell in love with your gaze
Precious like gems
Unlock the secrets in my mind
Dive into my heart
For you I'll write countless sonnets
Your lips like pillow of rosy gold
In this beaming alley
You lit a sparkle into my heart
You are my forever muse
Guiding my heart into bliss
Your voice charms angels choir
Your smile offering me
A lifetime of happiness
We are budding lovebirds
In this glorious venue
Our True Love reached the light
Of a shimmering future
Awaiting us

Letter for thee

In this splendorous dawn
I poured my heart into this letter
'My love' I wrote
As my heart is skipping beats
Such love as ink shaped
Letters for you to read
My saddened heart began to speak
For I miss you dearly
The flow of my ink
Alight with my deepest affection
In this moment
I wish I could shield you
From life's harshness
May my words unfold happiness
For your kindest soul
I long for your luminous smile
Swept away by the thought of you
Smiling at the words
My enamored soul has spoken
In this enveloppe
Sealed is my great love for thee
When the night is cold
The very thought of you
Sets my heart ablaze
Your letter, my candle
Amidst the abyssess of loneliness
Saying your name
Like a wish upon a star
For I feel your love from afar
In this enveloppe
Here I sealed my infinite love for thee

A Royal gleam

In this moonlit abode
Your smile sets my heart ablaze
Something wonderful lays within
As I gently caress your chin
Our hearts joined as one
Shaping blissful waves
In a sea of blankets
Our hearts begin to flutter
From a long embrace
Upon the softness of your lips
A warm kiss placed
'Be my Queen' I gently whisper
For my heart is your kingdom
Your brave allure saved me
From the darkest dungeons
In this moment of pure clarity
You become my life's essence
The stars take the shift from the sun
My heart takes delight in your love
You are the jewel in my crown
Entwined endeavors, we share
Your loving voice,my armor
As I lay with you my King
In your arms I want to reside
Happiness and Loyalty
Shall be our glorious throne
Crowned with peace and light
Make me your Queen
We shall prosper endlessly
Our heartbeats a sensual flow

Setting our worlds aglow
Our Royal allure
Shall reign this town
Our Love's seal, a beaming crown
Elations we give will last forever
Our union, a royal gleam
Emanating from us
The blaze of our enamored eyes
Defying the moon's beam
As I rejoice in your mighty warmth

An Afterglow

Loving whispers
Bodies intertwined like tangled wires
I find the place to lay my head
As our freckles align like constellations
Pressed against your skin
Entangled limbs
As to where you and I begin
You woke my sleeping senses
And warmed me to the bone
Together we move as one
In the splendid moment
I see moonlight dancing in your eyes
Together in the afterglow
Locked in love's sweet embrace
You're the starlight
In between my midnight eyes
Our Love's ballet
Crowned with splendor
Afterglow lover's blush
Passionate blood rush
I lose myself in your beam
Our fingers lock like magnets
Blending into one
I'm yours and you're mine
Your skin, the canvas
My fingertips, the paintbrush
Every touch, every glide upon it
Create a mark unlike any other
Writing our tale
Lulling you into dreams with my fingers

Waking you when sunlight creeps up the sheets
Our hearts and breaths in sync
Laying in the afterglow
Longing to paint our lives
In splendid memories
Days filled with bliss and passion
Sun shining on our tangled silhouettes
Our Love's ballet, an endless glow

A whirl of chances

On a sunlit day, his eyes landed on a vivid soul
Unlike any other
The gaze of his strange mysterious eye
Waking her heart to a sudden glow
She looked at him with star-flecked eyes
She found in his face, a familiar grace
Beaming smiles
Made sparks circle their silhouettes
Binding their fates for eternity
An undying love
Written in the moonlit sky
Their names engraved in each other's hearts
Like the endless sheen of stars
His coming stirring her soul
As the ocean is stirred by the wild's storm
On a piece of paper, he shouts his sheer love for her
Climbing to feel her embrace
Green Emerald eyes embracing his soul
Lips colliding into solmen bliss
He brought her the balm of heavenly calm
With a peace slowly crowning her life
Opening their hearts into a whirl of chances
They became each other's balance
Kissing each other's darkness
Admiring the beauty underneath
Facing roaring seas
Two broken souls became one
Meeting of two destined lovers
Stirring bliss into one another's hearts
His words taking her to a magical realms

A place where love conquers deepest fears
In the sweet dim of the falling night
She found him at her side writing verses of their love
With the invisible ink of his tongue
Letting a little bit of himself into her soul
Like a gentle whisper
As his arms hold her ever closer

A Reflection

The day I met you
You tempted me like an empty page
For I knew you and I
Were destined to write a tale
Filled with love, art and light
I instantly knew
You are the gift and the love
I always longed for
Through all your scars
I see a light
Your eyes shimmering from afar
Your presence,a precious sunlight
Healing my past wounds
Shall I compare you to a summer's day?
Let me compare you to the seven skies
For now you are mine
My heart has painted the beauty of your soul
You draw treasures to the canvas of my mind
Your reflection in the mirror
Outshines the lunar delight
My love, you are the soul of my art
The glow of your skin
Outshines the sunset's hues
Your silhouette, beautiful
Like polished clay
To my gaze
You gloriously shine so bright
An can be seen from afar
Only I, can see you like a lighthouse
Basking on the perpetual beauty

Of the world you have given me
My love, you are my muse
Guiding me to a beaming path
Filled with greatness
The day I met you
I knew we were written in the stars
You shaped my world
For now, the Moon swoons at our Love

I am, You are

You defeat the sun's light
I am the spilled ink on a page
You are the art next to it
I am the icy face-slapping wind
You are my warm summer breeze
Your eyes brighter than the stars light
Your voice prettier than every symphonies in the world
Than any nature's sounds
Every word you articulate, my sweet lullaby
My eyes soaking in your beauty
Oh you're a sight for sore eyes
As I rush towards you
No more words are spoken
My lips collide with yours
Creating our own language
Of Blissful love
You taste like cherries on top of milkshakes
Your lips are red roses overwashed with dew
Glistening in delight
Your tongue, full with the nectar of love
For you are my white dove
Guiding me in the clouds of bliss
I am the dying flower, you are the rain
I am the dark sky, you are the moon
I am the story, you are the poetry
I want to embrace your soul
Like the waves meet the shore

A Lunar Majesty

By this moonlit place
You are my lunar majesty
A constellation of emotions
Radiating in my heart
So ever brightly
Sand soft beneath our feet
The aura of our love
Defying the moon's sheen
The brightness of our cheeks
Shaming the countless stars above us
Fingertips tracing bliss
Whispers of love vows
Filling this night
With an otherworldly glow
For you are my life partner
Your soul binded to mine
My crown shall be yours to take
To possess
Our love sheds a luminescence unlike any other
Many-splendored kisses
Weaving the beaming thread
Of a beautiful tale
Our love story
By this moonlit place
We are each other's stellar majesty
As I crown you with the aura
Of my endless love
The soft touch of your lips
Flourishing my soul

With the brightest light
Defeating any darkness
For bliss is the seal
Of our entwined sparkling crown

In this sunlit café

'I wish we could just go' said I
Gazing at the perfect green glow
Of your splendid eyes
Our hands intertwined
Tangled fingers find their place
Lacing like zippers
Our voices, tracing love whispers
Casting a perfect day glow
In this sunlit café
Enamored voices shaping dreams
Long gone are the screams
When we're together
Stars are within reach
As our energy grows
An energy made of sparkles
The melody of our melded bodies
Resonates within our hearts
Creating a perfect symphony
A moment of beauty
When I hold your hand
Desires turn into Reality
Your soothing voice, my clarity
Together we'll run away
We'll be each other's homes
Among an array of places
The sun has set on another day
Our stress fading away
The ghostly wind blows through silent trees
As we ride by
We bathe in each other's light

Feeling your warmth flowing through me
Above the whitest clouds our spirits would glide
Kissing, strolling, swaying together
We write beautiful words together and compose
The finest symphony of love
Every blissful shared kisses
Giving birth to a glowing rose
Taking us to infinite galaxies
Of endless possibilities
While we soar among the stars
In this sunlit café
Enamored voices shaping dreams
This soft kiss you place in my lips
Burns with passion
The light in your eyes
Carries me across the deepest oceans
Takes me to the realm of our shared dreams
Where constellations shine for us
For now
In the distance fields are burning
The wind howls
There is no speech, only hearts speaking
There are no words, only hearts spilling
Our breathing falls in sync to a rhythm
Known only to the cosmos
At the end of our inhales
There you are
There I am
You and I painters of our fantasy
In this sunlit café

Sunset Hearts

High above the fading light
Of a brilliant early sunset
I take a big breath
Of that sumptuous air
My toes painted by the beaming sand
As I gaze into your sublime allure
Painted by the sun's golden hues
Dazzled by the light you cast
I pull your smile deep in my heart
And finally can breathe
In this moment
Gazing at you
The rebirth of freshly dewed dreams
Endowed with your sublime allure
Like a glowing gem
Amidst a moonlit sand
For you are the sky
I am the restless sea
Endlessly drawn to you
In this instant
The sun rays casting pink hues
The sunset of you reflects within me
As you are painted over with stars
Lover of mine
Your silhouette
Painting the color of romance
The color of my finest dreams
In the seabed
My love you are the sunset
I am the blushing sky

Mesmerized by your stance
Among this painting of golden hues
And silky clouds
I hear your heart beating with mine
Through the restless waves
Our hearts are set as one

Hope Thoughts

I live by the quote 'Where there's life, there's hope'. Hope is this beaming particle flowing around and coming to us when we call it. How to call it? By following your inner light and feeding on positive thoughts. Hope gives us wings, Hope gives us purpose, Hope gives us joy, Hope gives us a fulfilled life. Hope is the seeds of our soul. I believe souls are made of light, the more we lose hope, the more this light fades away. Always the path of hope, for YOU are destined to shine bright like the stars.

The following poems embody the most fragile petal of my thoughts when I was facing constant battles to keep my inner light in the darkest chapters of my life.

I always see cherry blossoms as a gift of Spring
A gift from life to show us
That new things, new chances, new opportunities
Are awaiting us
As the new season is among us
I am and forever will be
A strong believer
In fate, in the beauty of signs
A flower blossoming
A shamrock or flower petals swaying in the blue sky
Colorful butterflies
All these precious signs
Are Nature's wink
To tell us that even though things perrish
Even though things become dull
There will always be new sparks
New colors
New flowers, new blossoms
In our lives
Admire Nature's wink
Take a deep breath
Embrace this pattern
Of eternal and soothing
Renewal
Rebirth as your own inner Spring
Let your soul flourish new blossoms
Let your mind free itself from the broken branches
Let your heart singing to new songs

In this dim moment
I wish I could fly above
Take some distance
See the world in a bird eye view
My inner hope is hanging
Like the moon in the night sky
I just have to find the strength
To reach it
To catch it
Hold it and never let go
Can you catch the stars?
No but in this moment
You can look up to them
So open your eyes
And seek Hope's light
Among this dark steam
Blurring your view
Grow your own wings
And take your greatest flight
Above the dark steam
And don't look back

Our true colors always end up shining
Through the darkness and dullness we can face
Never give up on finding this glimmer of light
You will be okay
Just like the sun always rises
Your spirit will be enlightened with joy again
For your spirit is an horizon
Embrace the change of this horizon
And you'll find balance
At a peaceful pace

And above all
Be kind
For Kindness is the greatest perk in life
It can take you anywhere
Send you to the moon
Without ever leaving the ground
It can save lives
Heal souls in the blink of an eye
In these hard times
Never fail at spreading kindness
In any way in any form
Let your words be stardust
Dazzling the darkest paths
You might think you wont change the world
You will change someone's world
Smile to people, smile to strangers
Beyond strangers, they are part of the world's soul
All of us are joined into one purpose
To seek peace and to find joy
In every living moment
Create your own world
With your own magic
Defeating darkness
With your smiles
Acts of generosity
Be kind
Be a healer
Of the World's soul

The broken will always be able to love harder
Than most
Once you've been in the dark
You learn to appreciate everything that shines
Going through dark moments
Gives a certain amount of wisdom
A powerful clarity
Showing the real value of a wound
A wound is the place where light enters you
It has been synonym of pain
But slowly it becomes hope's seal
The seal of your inner light
And inner strength
The broken will always shine brighter
In his own way
The broken will always see clearer than most
For he has experienced the lack of light
And cherishes the tiniest speck of stardust
This world has to offer

Life is just a painting
Draw the lines with hope
Erase the mistakes with tolerance
Dip the brush with a lot of patience
And color it with love
Be a painter of love
When darkness falls
We can curl up with fear or turn on the lights
Be brave, love deeply, shine brighter
Let your inner light be the brush
Spreading love and colors when all is is dull
Let your words be a golden thread
Full of hope and faith in this world

For the sun always rises
You will get better
You will overcome the storms
Shine your own light
Don't let the dullness of others
Destroy your inner fest of colors
Fly away to a brighter sky
Where 'imagine' turn into reality
Build a better spirit
To heal the the soul of the world
To set the flame of hope ablaze
Mend your thoughts
For your happiness depends on the colors within your thoughts
We are stars wrapped in skin
The light you're seeking,has always been within
Darkness turns this light into a thin veiled spark
Fighting its way through the utter dark
You always been special
Let your inner light thrive
To pave your way to the wings of joy
Slowly enwrapping you
Fly away to this new horizon
Trace stars
Shape them into a constellation of your hopeful words
To show you the way when it's dark

Never apologize for burning too brightly
Or collapsing into yourself
Every night
That is how the stellar realm works
We are all made of stardust
Your emotions, thousands exploding stars
Leading to the prettiest constellations
In the sky of your life
Stars are meant to shine
Their light fades away at times
Much like yourself
For you are a stellar realm in progress
Your light is within reach
You just have to find the right path
You are a star
In a constantly changing sky

Your soul is a vessel
Fill it up
With kindness
And good intentions
Set your heartbeats
Into a hymn of hope
Hold tight to Love's rope
Where faith
Is your Heart's nest

Let your hope
Not your hurts
Shape your future
Let your belief in the greater good
Shape the horizon of your life
Let your hope reach
The zenith of your soul
Let hope be the sun rays of your days
Leave your hurts
At your past threshold
Gaze into your future
Laced with the thread of light and joy
Let your beaming smile
Be the seal of your
Everlasting hope

To see a world in a grain of sand

And a heaven in a Wild Flower

Hold infinity in the palm of your hand

And Eternity in an hour

For when the cold strikes

Look for the burning embers of your fiery soul

Sift through the ashes

In search of the spark

Igniting your grand mind

Lit up your heart

With the sparkle of your fiery soul

Guiding you into the greatest winds of life

Be a wind flower

Defying the spirit of a wildflower

Let the storms of life

Shape the embers of your soul

Into a magnificent diamond in the rough

Hope is the place where your hearts
Longs to go
Hope is the person you want to know
Hope is the feeling that carries you through
Hope is the abode of your soul
Hope knows no fear
Hope dares to blossom
Even inside the abysmal abyss
Hope secretly feeds
And strengthens
It is the thing with feathers
That perches in your soul
It is a sparkle
A traveler
Eager to meet you
It is a sunbeam
Warming our hearts for an instant
It is a sweet companion
We wish we could have by our sides
Forever
But Hope is meant to come and go
When our light from within
Thrives
It welcomes us with a warm embrace

Self thoughts

Self, yourself such a simple and yet powerful word embodying the entirety of Life as a whole. Yourself is what carries you through, it is what guides you in this journey called life. Yourself is meant to be cherished, meant to flourish and glow. Yourself is the past, the future and the present. It is the light of your truth and yet sometimes you tend to stray and sway among the darkest plains. Awaken yourself, birth yourself. For YOU are a gift to yourself, give this gift to the world, let your inner light expand its horizons. We tend to think that life is hard, when in truth it is how we envision ourselves that shapes the width of our hurdles.

If we cherished ourselves the self as we cherish treasures, life would be a peaceful stroll with some rain along the way.

Magic mind to slow unwind
A deep sigh to reflect
Balanced soul
So sweet and kind
A breath of self respect
Golden love to cure the soul
A patience to achieve
A peace to make the shoulders
Roll and make the heart believe

Carving myself
Like the finest sculptures
Rooted in strength and light
My heart is being filled with the freshness of a rose garden
My body is being splashed by sparkling crystals of water
And sprinkled with speckles of colors
My senses are caressed by sweet air breezes
My soul is drowned in the glittery ocean of love
I emerge alight with self-love
In a perfect effervescence
Where I shape my soul's essence
Into a beautiful symphony
Of love and light

I am a daydreamer
With fuming emotions
I am a wind in motion
An open book
Eager to be read and discovered
A book written with happiness
Words, thoughts and flying dreams
I am a landscape full of steams
My soul holds the four seasons' hues
I ride the waves of intensity
I touch the stars in remote prose
Wandering the vast expanses without close
Wherever my mind goes, it goes
I am a narrative that flows from within
I am words of golden hymns
Paving the way to salvation
My wings are inked words
A message of flames
Like water I flow
Like the stars I glow
What am I?
A fragment of your luminescent mind
For every mind has its luminescence
You just have to cultivate the right sparkles

A flower does not think of competing
With the flower next to it
It just blooms on its own
Spreading its own shades of colors
Beauty blooms from within
Focus on nourishing your inner blossoms
With the light surrounding you
Competing is not the path to take
Sun's rays, moon's beam
Shall be your one and only companions
Into your journey of self-realization
Rejoice in your own colors and shapes
Bloom on your own

She turned her cants into cans
Her dreams into plans
Planted her own gardens
Ornated her soul with the flowers
She picked for herself
Magic and mystery hung around her
In perfect symmetry
She breathed in prose
And let out poetry
In every words she pronounced
Painted her own glory
Towards self-love and joy
She turned dark thoughts into flowers
Spinned her inner darkness into a golden thread
Guiding her through the high and lows
Of her journey

One's mind is shaped like a dandelion flower
So fragile yet so precious
Dandelion shaped mind blooming its sparks
Giving birth to a luminescent horizon
Defying the Northern Lights
For life is a field meant to be flourished and nourished
Cultivate your own garden
Pick the right sparkles meant to grow
On the soil of your spirit
Make of your mind
A color-filled
Light-filled garden
Water your doubts with kindness
Let blossoms of belief and hope
Take over the dark branches that may grow
Make of your mind a high spirited tale
Meant to rise and shine brighter
Day after day

A whirlwind of broken glass
She landed on the grass of a meadow
Draped with a white dress
She became a tigress in spirit
Right there, her fierce journey began
Raven-haired princess
Beautiful curls whirling in the air
Running for her safety
She met her infinity
Embracing her fate
Her soul, endowed with sheer kindness
Her path, adorned with elegance
Delicate touch, healing presence
She became a Lady of Grace
Her heart taken into a realm of emotions
Among an abode of darkness
Her light spirit, a shooting star among the dusk
Healing wounds, mending souls
Battling her inner demons with the power of Love
Her words, a splendor of wisdom
Her mind, a garden of wonders
Adorning fellow souls with seeds of light
For she has the soul of a tiger
Filled with ardent desire
Spreading vivid sparks
Evolving into a dragonfly
A Dragonfly in Amber
Like a precious stone
Carved on a golden soil

Her mind, a secret garden
Full of blooming seeds
Feeding her soul with creativity
Diving into pages
Crossing thousands seas of inspiration
Her mind full of devotion
To discover buried treasures
Beneath golden parchments
Setting sail to live adventures
She smiles at the sight of shooting stars
Her imagination, a pure treasure
Enlightening all the paths she crosses
Leaving a mark in her heart
The mark of a true believer
Being endlessly clever
Her creativity, a glowing phoenix
A fierce revival like the leaves in Autumn
Pink blossoms in Spring
Living her dreams brilliantly
Spinning gold with her mind
Writing beautiful tales
Living in a classic manor
In all her splendor

Meditation thoughts

Flying is a fantasy for the human soul. This power is within reach with the act of meditation, meditation is the soul of life, it evolves the power of your thoughts, magnifies your inner light and joy into blissful clouds. The following thoughts are inspired by my journeys as I was contemplating the facets of life.

Ornated book covers
Walking in the greatest meadows of Life
Whispering, shimmering hues of wisdom
Ornated book covers
Healing the world's fevers
A stance so pure so stellar
To one's mind
Wrinkles like constellations
On a night sky
Each bearing a story
A century filled with ordeals
Pain, strife, chaos
Relief, joy, love
Loss,tears,birth
The abode of their spirit

This is the color of a sunflower
Bright beautiful colors dazzling your eyes
The smooth flower petals in your hand
Holding eternal beauty in your palms
The sweetest taste for the bees
The crown of blooming love stories
Colors that warm your heart
Making you feel whole in this instant
Hearing birds chirping when Beauty arises
This is Nature's Bouquet
Unfolding a blissful ballet made of fresh wind
Sun rays and flowing petals

Cherry pink blossoms
Soft palette of pastel hues
Scents of spring in bloom
The sun shines down
Pink flowers grow softly
Birds flutter around the branches
Giving me a tranquil feeling
Breathing in the sweet scent of petals
My heart filled with joy
My mind inhabited by Spring's wisdom

I look up at the starry sky
Which is so solemn holy and pure
The severe and awe-inspiring justice
Makes me filled with deep love and awe of it
I look up at the starry sky
Which is so free and serene
The broad beamy horizon
Provides the place wheremy soul rests and nestles
In the graceful embrace
Of the starry sky's breeze

In the end books may well be the only true magic the human soul can hold into.

I believe books have souls
I believe the human heart seeks its sparkles in books
They embody an infinity unlike any other
Books hold the concept of forever
The power of ink and a mind can trace endless magic waves
It shapes changing tides in one's life
Let's all hold into the true magic books have to offer
For they are the mind's constellations
Pages making us travel miles
Within a second
In a heartbeat
Books, infinite realms
With endless treasures

The setting sun
Ten miles of snow
Changing colors
Shades of sunlit skies
Long winter snow
Gives way to warming sun
Weak sun nudges in some heat
Trees eager for Springtime

Change your narrative
Let it flow with ands and get rid of the but
Dance with fear don't let it define who you are
What you want to achieve
Bad ideas or rippled crippled papers
Are not a fatality
They shape the sparks of your mind
Be the narrator of your life
Type with serenity and positivity

Teaching is the art of painting progress...

My dearest pupils
With joy I teach you
The wonders of a language
So ever vibrant
Your energy, my daily sunshine
Your smiles give me joy
Jolly minds
To be inspired
To be moved
My dearest pupils
Your words bring sparks to my mind
Set my inspiration
To a positive pace
Where we can build a safe place
Filled with generosity
And serenity
In the shape of a book
Where your words pour light
Into the pages of this year

Strength is like a footprint
Meant to be molded over time
Strength is the dna of your soul
Each hurdle you go through
Shape your soul's imprint
Each wound carries a light
Showing you the right way
Like a lighthouse from within
When angry waves seem to reach you
Know you're not alone
Stand in the wind and breathe with each gust
Grab the canoe and take the oars
Defy the roars of the highest tempests
Pull yourself against the tide
Feel the salt water on your cheeks
Sweet horizons shall shine your way
Draw your strength from the stars above
Your courage from the clouds
Stellar strength
Be your body's seal
Filled with beaming scars
Defeating dark hues
Strength is a footprint
Meant to be molded
And cherished deeply

Butterflies can't see their wings
They can't see how truly beautiful they are
But everyone else can
For you are a butterfly
Meant to fly away in all glory and beauty
Adorned with colorful wings
Painting colorful waves in the blue sky
In the darkest moments you crawl
In the brightest moments you fly to shinny horizons
Your soul is destined to a glorious flight
Where gazes are dazzled
By your luminescent spirit

Brighter than the blinding flares
Of the sun, shimmering outward with power
Of thousand of stars
Yet comforting, yet soft
Filled with oceans crashing and wild
Rushing under a powerful storm
Yet still, yet calm
Filled with wonder and curiosity
Yearning for the unknown
Yet wise, yet content
Eyes so wide, so deep, filled with delicate roses
The power of mighty warriors
Elegant as Venus' flowing dress
Filled with fiery souls
Filled with beauty
With you
The gleam of knowledge

Memories are like a library
I long to run through the archives of my memory
Finding various books with titles
Embodying the days I have lived
Days of shimmering sunshine
Days of raging storms
I browse through myriads of colors
Only to realize I found myself
I found that these books
Contain my walking dreams
My fears, my hopes
Memory reminds us of our essence
The essence that brings tranquility to one's soul
On a stormy day
An essence that reminds us of our rightful path
In the library of my memories
I see dusty book covers
Holding my greatest battles
Beyond mere dust
I see star dust
Witness of my courage

When a new year comes
We say happy new year
I say Happy Wonderful You
The new year is nothing but a soil
A horizon afresh
With numbers changing
But you, yourself
Crossed more than a decade
Polished yourself day after day
Set your fate aglow
With fleeting wishes
For this new year is a new chapter
You are the golden book cover
You are the warrior at heart
A beaming soul
A brand new chapter is in sight
Many battles, you will encounter
Face them with bravery
To turn them into milestones
Of your armor
Shield yourself with hope
For the future is a blurry horizon
Filled with wondrous depths
Set your heart to a new pace
Let hopeful words rise on your breath
For your days
Are a multitude of polished memories
Into a grand constellation
Some days are meant to shine
Others are meant to fade

Sweetest gestures shall revive your soul
Sweetest thoughts revive your heart
On this new year ahead
Do not dim your light
With dark clouds
Don't wait for Christmas
To twinkle
Let this new year
Be an endless Ode
For a better you
Let your thoughts
Turn into a beautiful symphony
Celebrating yourself
You are enough
A diamond in the rough
Happy Wonderful You!
Gaze at your fate
With a heart ablaze with joy
Tranquil moments
To ease your soul
Happy Wonderful You!

I am immensely desired
I am in the sky
In the water ever so blue
In the earth's hues
I am from within
From every horizon
I can be heard everywhere
I am seen in the sunlight
In the trees
I endlessly roam
In the air
Within every living beings
Sometimes I am bare
Ornated, adorned
I touch hearts
What am I?
Sparkles in the air?
Starlight?
Perhaps
For I burst, I blossom gracefully
Unbound by gravity
I am what's echoing within you
When your heart's a hurricane
I am here to sprinkle it
With serenity and bliss
Your soul longs for me
You are elated at my sight
I am Beauty
Beneath your skin
Between your thoughts

Within your soul
For you can keep me forever
Unless you let me fully enter within your thoughts
I am an ocean of emotions
By my side you shall thrive
Bloom gloriously
And embark on a unique journey
Into the greatest realm of all
Yourself

She is the city lights
The stars
The candlelights
Everything else that makes darkness
Look beautiful
She brews courage
Seeing the stars of possibility
Defying the law of gravity
With her inner strength
She twinkles in the distance
Her soul, a vast horizon of wondrous beauty
Her scars cast an array of light
Much like the stars she's a stubborn creature
For stars fill the night sky
And conceal some greater morning
Her flickers of hope
Turning into golden fibre glitters and gleams
Interwoven in the night sky
Her mind flourishes in the dark
Blossoms giving birth to unique sparkles
Guiding her into salvation
Celestial thoughts bringing beauty
Her tears,specks of stardust
To all the paths she walks in
Much like her
We are all beautiful
Even if sometimes we feel lonely
We are like the moon
Even in the darkness we still shine so bright
From within

Life is filled with beauty
Even when we close our eyes
Our gazes hold multitude of stars
Fest of colors
Much like phosphenes
Those blinking dots
When you rub your eyes
The colorful ones
That dance around alluringly
You are much like phosphenes
A vast array of colors
Destroying boundless darkness
I immerse myself in your beauty
Sweet serenity
A blissful feeling
A gift to one's heart

With these thoughts alight, I hope I inspired you. I hope you will seek sparkles for your mind in my secret garden.

Dear reader you read my words inked on a paper, beyond reading I hope you lived and imagined these words.

The paper was the podium of my creative expression filled with depth. All I ever dreamed of was to inspire people and pour light into the world's soul with the greatest magic of all: WORDS.

Here is one last poem dedicated to you dear reader:

Precious soul

From the opposite side of this creative realm
In the palm of your hand lays my secret garden
Thoughts I have nourished and cherished for a decade
This poem is written for you
Whenever you're sad and look in the mirror
Remember you're a stellar realm in progress
You are a luminescent mind
You are a dandelion flower
Beaming and soaring
In the prettiest skies
You are a rare flower
Bearing your own seal
You are unique
And destined to wonderful things
For as the stars shine bright
Your soul is meant to dazzle minds
From now on
This secret garden
Filled with thoughts alight
Shall be your source
Of inspiration and serenity
Like a flowing river
Like a waterfall
Drink from it,refresh your soul
I hope
Wholeheartedly
From I,to you
-Kawtar Elmrabti

Printed in the USA
CPSIA information can be obtained
at www.ICGtesting.com
LVHW011931120724
785355LV00001B/349